3 *Plans As They Are and As They Might Be*, Kate Finning & Guillermo Fernández-Abascal
5 *Making Plans*, Jonathan Sergison
9 *A Genealogy of Generic Plans*, Irina Davidovici
15 *Best Laid Plans ...*, Alan Pert

23 Esch Sintzel Architekten
31 Lütjens Padmanabhan Architekt*innen
39 Conen Sigl Architekt*innen
49 Karamuk Kuo
59 Edelaar Mosayebi Inderbitzin Architekt*innen

Plans As They Are and As They Might Be

Kate Finning & Guillermo Fernández-Abascal

The floor plan is the architectural project that most directly impacts our daily lives. As such, the floor plan is the primary project of housing. However, as architects and teachers, we find that the domestic floor plan is rarely the focus of architectural theory, discussion or debate.[1] In contrast, the floor plan holds primacy in the procurement, sale and rental of dwellings.[2] This misalignment of interests results in the dwelling plan becoming the jurisdiction of developers, bureaucrats and real estate-agents who claim expertise in the vacuum left by architects. Proof of this oversight can be found in the primarily functionalist and quantifiable language that dominates the description of domestic floor plans, which results in a secondary effect: our imagination is also captured by the market.

But what of the *art* of the domestic floor plan? The narrowing of floor plan design to quantifiable criteria is a reduction of its material potential. Spaces rarely exist in binaries and yet we are taught to design through oppositional concepts such as served vs servant, open vs closed, public vs private and indoor vs outdoor spaces. In reality, architectural elements and formal motifs define the character of spaces through degrees. We might imagine that the rooms of a plan exist on a qualitative spectrum, from open to closed, dark to light, or wet to dry. When conceiving of plans in this way, we allow for considerations such as hierarchy, arrangement, composition and thermal delight, in addition to the pragmatics of use and construction. It may be more difficult to describe, but this qualitative approach is no less precise.

In his treatise on the English residence, Robert Kerr outlined his general considerations for the domestic plan to include criteria such as comfort, convenience, spaciousness, compactness, salubrity, cheerfulness, elegance, importance and ornamentation.[3, 4] With a belief that the qualities that are most difficult to define might just be the most important, we want to build literacy in the qualitative aspects of the floor plan. We want to think not of circulation, but of a sense of arrival; not of function, but of use; not of floor area, but of the number of, and quality of, rooms. These are not new ideas. In fact, they are very old, but it is worth reminding ourselves that the room precedes function and that use need not be singular.

The architects included in this publication suggest that the task of housing is to balance a

1 Some exceptions to this can be found in the theory and teaching of Pier Vittorio Aureli, Xavier Monteys and Martin Steinmann, as well as the texts and lectures of Jonathan Sergison and Stephen Bates. Unfortunately much of the work of Monteys and Steinmann is yet to be translated into English.

2 Here we refer to both affordable and luxury dwellings, and everything in between.

3 Robert Kerr, *The Gentleman's House: or, How to Plan English Residences, from the Parsonage to the Palace*, London: John Murray, Albemarle Street, 1864.
Kerr's text was introduced to a contemporary audience by Robin Evans in his essay 'Figures, Doors and Passages', in which he included a diagram of Kerr's Bearwood residence, presenting the plan as a binary of circulation and living spaces. See 'Figures, Doors and Passages', *Architectural Design*, 1978, 48: p. 273.

strong spatial determinacy with an indeterminacy of use. What these determined spatial qualities might be, and how to design them, is what excites us most, and is the reason why we study ideal dwellings. To begin, we have restricted ourselves to five.

4 [EDITOR'S NOTE] The frequency with which Evans' text is cited reflects the lack of domestic floor plan theory since. For us Evans' essay is an introductory but by no means exhaustive account. Although beyond the scope of this publication, it is worth noting that while Evans declared the first recorded corridor to have been designed around 1597 in Beaufort House, Chelsea (Evans, pp. 271-272), Kerr includes earlier examples such as Oxburgh Hall, Norfolk, 1482 (Kerr, p. 41 and Plate 7). Evans cited Kerr's text elsewhere in his essay, so we are curious to know what led to this oversight.

A Note on Swissness

When embarking on a close study of Swiss housing one quickly confronts the argument of Swiss exceptionalism.[5] Instead, we imagine these five plans as a shortcut to better housing in Australia, without neglecting our own lineage.[6] In Switzerland, literacy in housing design has been built over generations.[7] The five architects of this publication studied, worked for, or were taught by Diener & Diener, Meili & Peter, Peter Märkli and many other good architects. We believe that a good average standard of housing can lead to nuances and refinement over time.

Just as a group of London architects (alongside Caruso St John, Tony Fretton, Florian Beigel and Sergison Bates) looked to Swiss architectural culture in the 1990s, we are a small group of Australian architects looking to Swiss plans to practise and teach the architecture of housing through a tradition that is revisited and refined over time.

5 Jack Self, 'The Master of Plans', *RUMOR*, Princeton University School of Architecture, 2019, 6.

6 There are local examples that we would like to include. Here we refer to many of the Art Deco and mid-century apartment plans in Sydney and Melbourne. See for example, Terry Sawyer, 'Residential flats in Melbourne: the development of a building type to 1950', The University of Melbourne Thesis (unpublished), 1982.

7 J. Lucan and M. Steinmann, 'Construcciones helvéticas: tema y variaciones. Helvetian Constructions: Theme and Variations', *AV. Monografias/Monographs*, 2001, 89: pp. 4-10.

Making Plans
Jonathan Sergison

Housing forms the dominant building programme in any city and is the task that architects most frequently engage with. It follows that the internal organisation of plans is critical. Although the façades of buildings contribute to urban decorum, it is apartment plans that affect the life of their residents and organise domestic life. As such, housing designers have a great responsibility to the city: their buildings add to the urban fabric through the arrangement of everyday life.

The development of plans is constrained by building regulations, client briefs and the requirements of the housing market although architects are often motivated by a desire to be original, experimentation is not generally sought by the parties funding a project. Any form of innovation carries the risk that an apartment won't sell or rent for the amount envisaged by the developer. In Switzerland's major cities the risk is less significant because the housing market is so buoyant. Currently in Zurich, the housing occupancy rate is more than 99 percent. It is difficult to find decent and affordable apartments, as demand is greater than supply. In more remote regions, the financial risks developers take are greater, and profit margins tighter.

In the period since the end of World War II, Switzerland has witnessed a remarkable flourishing of architectural production. The architectural culture of this small alpine country is unmatched in its rigour and consistently high quality. Despite its relatively limited territory, it must be understood as a series of regions that, at different times, have hosted moments of originality that have had significant influence: Geneva in the 1950s and 60s, Ticino in the 1970s and 80s, Basel in the 1990s, the Graubünden in the early 2000s and, in recent years, Zurich. Admittedly, this is a simplification of a much more complex and layered map of creativity and originality, which also involves some competitiveness between the regions, and a certain amount of local pride in their architectural production.

The housing produced in the last 70 years is experimental but never to the extent that it risks the level of failure that has occurred in many European countries. Architects are well trained and knowledgeable about construction. Swiss society is also intrinsically collectivist and decisions that relate to buildings are widely discussed by the communities that will be affected by them. Architecture is subject to democratic processes: voting on projects happens at either a municipal, cantonal or federal level, depending on the scale and significance of the project. Furthermore, housing projects and any publicly funded building are managed through the competition system, which is well organised and accepted as the best way to achieve quality. It is the principal means for architects to gain work and it is therefore very competitive. It is also a barometer of shifting trends and directions in architecture.

The City of Zurich has produced a substantial publication about the housing competitions it has organised, documenting entries to housing competitions in the region.[1] Projects are invariably shown as plans, and the overall result is exceptional both in terms of quality and quantity, revealing the shifting interests and preoccupations of architects in Zurich in recent years. The protagonists of this publication, who are generally Zurich-based practices, have certainly contributed to this collective endeavour. They are keen students of the work of their colleagues and of earlier generations of housing architects, which they have re-interpreted in their own way.

At an event initiated recently by Irina Davidovici and Tom Avermaete, most participants (who included Jeannette Kuo, Maria Conen, Oliver Lütjens and Thomas Padmanabhan among others) declared that *The House and the City* by Martin Steinmann and Roger Diener was the publication that had exerted the greatest influence on them. This is not surprising. The Basel office of Diener & Diener has produced the most exceptional body of work, which includes a wide range of housing projects. Their plans demonstrate a tremendous sense of rigour: they are not spectacular but immensely disciplined. Great attention is given to their flexibility and their capacity to be good homes. Rooms have good proportions and corridors are generally avoided because they are not an efficient use of space; the living room is generally in the middle of an apartment, with secondary rooms connecting to it. Everywhere good planning and generosity are on display. But there are also architectural demands that go beyond the need to create a good place to live. Diener & Diener's plans are orderly and well composed, never at the expense of usability of the apartment but as a matter of personal ambition. The younger generation of Zurich architects is aware of the work of this older practice; they have studied their plans and learnt lessons that they have then applied in different ways.

Another source of interest in recent years has been the post-World War II architecture of northern Italy. We can see the influence of the

1 Jeremy Hoskins and Tanya Reimer, eds., *Floor Plan Manual: Non-Profit Housing (Revised and enlarged edition)*, Editions Hochparterre, City of Zurich Planning Office, Zurich, 2020.

plans of architects like Luigi Caccia Dominioni in the work of Zurich architects in their loose geometries, and somewhat organic plan arrangements. While Italian architects working in Milan in the 1950s and 60s were creating homes for bourgeois tastes and needs, their work is relevant because the housing standards in Switzerland are generally quite generous.

In 2006, we entered a competition in Geneva with Jean-Paul Jaccaud, whose practice is based in the city. The brief for the competition for the municipality was to create a crèche and community space, as well as social housing. Rather unusual for a Swiss competition, it did not stipulate the number nor the mix of apartments. At the time we were happy to enjoy the freedom that we saw in Swiss housing standards after years of working with very tight housing constraints in London. On winning the competition we heard from the Geneva City Architect that one of the reasons our project was selected was that we proposed twice as many apartments as our Swiss colleagues. In the process we learnt a lesson about codes and conventions and realised that our education in housing in the United Kingdom was not altogether a bad thing – especially in the context of a city that needs to accommodate more people. Geneva is currently the densest of Swiss cities. What they all have in common is a restriction from building in the surrounding countryside. Swiss cities must densify housing within the existing municipal limits to prevent urban sprawl, which may threaten land used for agricultural production, or natural landscapes as a form of amenity.

The need to densify inevitably leads to a questioning of space standards and the amount of habitable area afforded to the residents of cities. It remains to be seen if this will in the future stifle creativity or yield alternative solutions and tighter plan arrangements. If the latter occurs, it may not in itself be a bad thing, given the growing need for urban housing.

The task architects will arguably need to address with greater urgency is the reuse of existing buildings, even those not originally built to support housing programmes. The current tendency to demolish and rebuild to a higher density is increasingly being questioned – not only in terms of heritage, but also lost embodied energy. While the creation of a new apartment building offers greater freedom, the repurposing of existing structures is more complex and demanding, although far more responsible in environmental terms. The practices included in this publication have already demonstrated their willingness to take on the challenge. The body of work amassed contains many examples of reuse and repurposing. In their professional activities as in their teaching, the architects demonstrate a commitment to a timely and critical revision of housing plans.

A Genealogy of Generic Plans
Irina Davidovici

The generic plan is one idea that distinguishes 'housing' from the archetypal 'house'. We could think of the generic plan as one that is hardly planned: it could be inhabited by anybody, in any manner, and at any time. In other words, it is a concept that could never be built, much like the 'primitive hut'. The generic plan, as a dwelling type, is based upon the inhabitant type, and both abstractions are based on the principles and forces of industrial mass production. And yet, what is often thought of as a generic housing plan is, in fact, rigidly predetermined – politically, economically, socially and not least ideologically. One should never let the serial logic that dictates housing configurations, and the universality that results from mass replication, conceal the actual rigidity of these invisible underlying structures.

In the 19th century, bourgeois reformers conceived of working-class dwellings as modular compartments, separating, firstly, different families and, secondly, members of the same family from each other. With this, they imposed their own middle-class values and behaviours upon the working-class population. Initially the effort was met with mixed reactions, and not only because higher rents tied the previously nomadic workforce to its places of employment. Another cause, as Robin Evans so compellingly demonstrates, was the hesitation with which the intended residents traded off commonality for privacy, and the freedom of the hovel, however squalid, for the supervision of the reformed, hygienic dwelling.[1] Henry Roberts' Model Dwellings prototype built for the 1851 Great Exhibition successfully encapsulated – and widely disseminated – a vision of the nuclear family that has underlined housing configurations ever since. It is indicative of its generic character that the plan of Roberts' housing prototype – two three-bedroom apartments on each floor, distributed around the central staircase with natural ventilation – was still largely recognisable in the modernist mass housing of the 1920s. One can hardly think of a more generic proposition, allowing any number of permutations and variations based on a limited set of social and economic premises.

In Switzerland, the generic nuclear-family plan introduced in the late 19th century and ratified by modernist architecture has enjoyed an honourable history. However, it seems almost redundant to group together the 'five good Swiss plans' discussed in this book under a national index, when their genetic data, so to speak,

1 Robin Evans, 'Rookeries and Model Dwellings', in *Translations from Drawing to Building and Other Essays*, vol. 2, Architectural Association, London, 1997, pp. 93-119, here pp. 110-111.

is culturally defined by a much wider Western context. The criteria for the value judgement of 'good' is equally intriguing and would require much detangling.[2] Should not the generic nature of the dwelling plans insulate them from micro-cultural specificities? Besides, none of these five plans – inventively thought out, carefully executed and generous to live in – can be thought of as bog-standard in the way so often associated with the notion of 'generic'. Nor do they at first glance, in terms of geometries and dispositions, seem to have much in common with one another. However, in viewing them in a well-established history of recent (German-) Swiss architecture, it is possible to inscribe them a specific common trajectory and sketch out a more recent historical genealogy of which they are – implicitly, inadvertently and inevitably – a part.

These five apartment plans were all designed between 20 and 25 years after the prominent Swiss architecture critic and historian Martin Steinmann postulated the 'neutralisation of the plan' in 1993.[3] According to Steinmann, the changing social, economic and cultural conditions at the end of the 20th century required the reassessment of the domestic plan, as inherited from the late 19th and early 20th centuries. The societal transformations allowed the co-existence of many different, equally valid, modes of living: not only the different types dictated by the nuclear family and collective living, but also at the level of the family itself – the interfaces between private and shared spaces, diurnal and nocturnal activities, and the (re-)integration of productive labour within the home. To respond to current demands, the plan needed to become 'neutral,' emptied of the pragmatic reformist zeal of the liberal bourgeoisie, as well as the economically grounded rationalisation of early 20th-century social-democrats.

In a debate published in the French-language journal *Faces*, Steinmann discussed this proposition with architects Michael Alder, Roger Diener, Meinrad Morger and Reiner Senn – leading German-Swiss practitioners of different generations, all with extensive housing design portfolios. Together, they questioned several tropes of bourgeois and modernist housing, namely the dichotomy of the served and serving spaces – and thus the reliance on corridors, the predetermined sizes and hierarchy of rooms – dictating the manner of their use, interfaces with external spaces, and the provision of balconies and loggias, private or shared. Using historical references as well as their own built projects, these architects explored current potentialities

2 For possible expansion on and partial answers to this question see Christophe Joud and Lorrain Beaudoin, 'Contemporary Swiss Housing: The Space Experiment', in Adam Jasper, ed., *House Tour: Views of the Unfurnished Interior*, Park Books, Zurich, 2018, pp. 80–91 and Bruno Marchand et al., *Contextes: le logement contemporain en situation*, EPFL Press, Lausanne, 2021.

3 'Typologies. Réflexions sur le logement contemporain. Débat entre Michael Alder, Roger Diener, Meinrad Morger, Reiner Senn et Martin Steinmann', in *Faces – Journal d'architecture*, no. 28 (Summer 1993), pp. 4–9.

for generic plans. They sought ways to render them as free as possible of the presumptions and values of their designers, as well as developers, public or private clients, and non-resident owners. The focus could then move on to the inhabitants as independent actors, free to adapt neutral, judgement-free apartments to their own ways of life. Roger Diener's words summarised the role of the architect in this project:

> We find ourselves at a crucial juncture. On the one hand, we notice that there's no such thing as a standard family, nor the standard needs of such a family. Needs change from one social group to another, even in Switzerland, and express themselves differently. On the other hand, we do not even know who the residents are. This means that rules according to which we have conceived our plans lose their significance, that we should abandon presumptions rooted in the 1920s (housing history). If we do not know the needs of inhabitants, we cannot address them in our plans. We should equip ourselves with new rules, which give us the freedom to consider things differently.[4]

By involving practitioners and giving voice to their concerns, Steinmann kept the notion of the 'neutral plan' apart from a purely theoretical sphere, arguing instead for its concrete implementation. New presumptions for housing design could already be perceived in the plans referred to in the discussion, which introduced (or re-introduced) scenarios for living we still see reflected in today's designs. Morger and Degelo's Müllheimerstrasse housing block, Basel (1989–1994), grouped modest flats around a generous internal, yet light-filled staircase, loosely based on Le Corbusier's Immeuble Clarté in Geneva. Two sizes of rooms, accessed through a short and wide corridor (not unlike a room itself) were expressed on the façade through identical full-height windows. Continuous galleries, of varying widths, wrapped around the building. In Michael Alder's Vogelbach housing complex in Riehen (1989–1992), flats are entered on a strong axis that would read as a corridor, were it not for the extensive glazing on one side, with rooms aligned on the opposite side, leading to a large kitchen-dining-living area. Loosely connected to the residential blocks are long, very generous loggias stacked on top of each other to create a quasi-autonomous perpendicular wing. Rainer Senn brought to the discussion a typical plan

4 Ibid, p. 9 (translation by the author).

in the residential district Burgfelderstrasse, Basel (1993), with a central access corridor and removable walls, allowing for the adaptation of each pair of flats to suit the circumstances of their inhabitants. And arguably the best-known of all is Diener & Diener's adjusted U-shaped apartment building in Warteck, Basel (1991–93, completed 1996), where the absence of balconies is compensated by roof terraces, both collective and individual. The double-aspect flats are accessed via a small vestibule, through large central living-rooms, onto which open the kitchens, bathrooms and two to three smaller rooms of identical sizes oriented towards the west and north.

Mostly completed in the early 1990s, these examples were embedded in the formative experiences of the younger professional generation featured in this book. It matters little that, or indeed whether these younger architects have read the article by Steinmann et al., since the projects it discusses were widely published, exhibited and were generally part of the discourse that had shaped them as architects at the time of their training. This is perhaps where the Swiss index becomes of significance – when considering the circulation of professional knowledge in the locally limited theatres of teaching and practice. The intimate ecology of students, teaching assistants and professors at ETH is – and remains, albeit to a lesser degree – strongly connected to a parallel hierarchy of practitioners and architects-in-training, which was perceptible in German-speaking Switzerland in the urban centres and suburbs where multi-family housing dominated as a type – Zurich and, particularly in the 1990s, Basel. That said, this knowledge – and the historical references that crop up – are hardly only Swiss and not even specifically so.

The features that distinguish the 'five good plans' of the present book from the abstract idea of the generic (modernist) plan are those that connect them to the discreet charm of the 19th-century bourgeois dwelling – for the middle, rather than labouring, classes. Indeterminate rooms suited to multiple functions, oversized or multiple doors and orientations, flowing or loosely compartmentalised spatial sequences, the proliferation of enfilades, the organisation of centripetal rooms around central internal hallways, the rejection of hierarchies in the size and dispositions of rooms are familiar themes in middle-class housing. They are particularly present in the post-war reinterpretations of the 'Italo moderno' invoked by Mosayebi in her presentation (introduced to younger generations by Marcel Meili and Markus Peter in their teaching at ETH, these buildings are known to most of her contemporaries from their common training). A cursory examination of the training and teaching of the authors – founding partners at Conen Sigl, EMI, Esch Sintzel, Karamuk Kuo and Lütjens Padmanabhan – reveals the complex discursive network connecting them to the previous generation of architects, whether as students, assistants or erstwhile employees. Considering the primacy accorded to residential architecture in Switzerland, both historically as well today or 30 years ago, these entanglements are not only professionally active, but also culturally reinforced. Correspondingly, the recent genealogy of the generic plan is enmeshed with the nature of recent Swiss architectural practice, and – closely related – the substance of Swiss architectural theory.

A Note on Height

Firstly, the generic plan is always an interior – unlike actual apartments in built buildings, whose haptic experience and real estate value are equally conditioned by location, approach and complementarity with a given setting. Secondly, even when considered as an 'unfurnished interior', the generic plan does not provide information about the height – and the natural light – which confer generosity and sociability even to small rooms. This conspicuous omission, briefly noted during the 1993 discussion by both Morger and Diener, was brought to the very core of the Swiss Pavilion installation at the 2018 Venice Biennale, entitled 'Svizzera 240: House Tour'.[5] While the 240 (cm) of the title referred to the standard height for residential spaces in German-Swiss building regulations, the exhibit subverted the abstract standard by playing with subtle and not-so-subtle shifts in scales. The result instilled in visitors feelings of estrangement and dysmorphia, close to an Alice-in-Wonderland experience. By drawing attention to the height, width, light, and perception of unfurnished residential spaces, the young curators – architects, artists and teaching assistants at ETH in Zurich – added an extra dimension to the Swiss genealogy of the two-dimensional generic plan.

5 The installation was curated by Alessandro Bosshard, Li Tavor, Matthew van der Ploeg and Ani Vihervaara and won the Golden Lion at the 2018 Biennale in Venice. See Adam Jasper, ed., *House Tour: Views of the Unfurnished Interior*, Park Books, Zurich, 2018.

Best Laid Plans ...[1]
Alan Pert

> Every plan is an agenda, and not just a tectonic programme, but a metaphorical and ideological one, too.[2]

The two-dimensional image that is the plan contains within it the instructions for the three-dimensional object that is the building. Every plan is also a solution to certain structural and spatial problems. While the elevation tends to pictorialise, the plan, section and structure integrate spatial ideas. Of the three, the plan is typically the most fundamental expression of architectural ideas. Although the differences amidst the selected 'Five Good Swiss Plans' are obvious, I am drawn to the common vocabulary of primary and secondary elements that shift and change – their slight modifications, peculiarities and variations – and how these then transform the apartment and the human activities within. Oskar Hansen might refer to these shifts as 'variable compositions', where the processes of life are highlighted by an architecture of 'backgrounds'.[3]

Hansen would go on to suggest that architectural structures are auxiliary to human activity and that the individual should be considered the co-author of the space. Even the best laid plans might be disrupted by the multiple events that unfold with the patterns of daily life – the paths traced by bodies through designed domestic space. Austrian architect and theorist Hermann Czech suggested that 'Architecture is background'.[4] Yet he also remarked: 'that doesn't mean it has to be inconspicuous, it can be precise or distinctive. Background also means that you can lean on it – and that it holds.'[5] As such, each of the plans in this publication can be read as backgrounds that are open to the unexpected, to the trivialities of daily life.

It is helpful to consider Robin Evans' thoughts on what plans signify, which he does in his seminal essay 'Figures, Doors and Passages'. He argues that:

> If anything is described by an architectural plan, it is the nature of human relationships, since the elements whose trace it records – walls, doors, windows and stairs – are employed first to divide and then selectively to re-unite inhabited space. But what is generally absent in even the most elaborately illustrated building is the way human figures will occupy it.[6]

The online discussion that took place at the

1 A proverbial expression used to signify the futility of making detailed plans when the ability to execute them is uncertain.

2 Marie-Ange Brayer, Langlands & Bell Exhibition Catalogue, 'Surrounding Time, 1993, Fonds Regional d'Art Contemporain du Centre Orleans France.

3 Hansen was a member of Team 10, the architectural group that formed the first critical voice against the modernist orthodoxy of the Athens Charter and the followers of Le Corbusier. In his Open Form theory, Hansen proposed parting ways with the model of the all-knowing expert. Hansen presented his Open Form theory at Team 10's founding meeting – the International Congresses of Modern Architecture (CIAM) in 1959 – and continued to develop it through projects on various scales: from exhibition designs, temporary pavilions and housing estates, to his Linear Continuous System, a project to establish decentralised cities running throughout Poland and the European continent. Regardless of the scale to which it was applied, the Open Form theory was intended to develop strategies of indeterminacy, flexibility and collective participation.

4 Eva Kuss, *Hermann Czech: An Architect in Vienna*, Park Books, Zurich, 2023, p.128.

5 Ibid, p.128.

end of the 'Five Good Swiss Plans' symposium reinforced that this group of architects are thinking about how people might inhabit the plan. Galvanised by a new spatial expression, they appear to be developing and moving away from the deterministic traditions of their ETH teachers who had established the rules of the game. Instead of seeing housing as a system within a larger aggregate form they are considering the contexts that they cannot control.

This publication presents a group of architects with a common agenda, a spatial-experiential point of view and a shared quest for complexity and richness of interior experiences. Four of the five case study apartment plans were presented innocent of furniture – the plans were emptied out to reveal the underlying structure and the primary elements of each of the domestic spaces. Each of the case studies allows the discipline of architecture to reclaim the interior.

When considering a vocabulary of primary elements, we might also reflect on how little the professional and academic realms have discussed the erasure of elements like the room, the cellar or the attic. In her 1934 book *Modern Housing* Catherine Bauer describes the development of interior space as something that was 'directed rather than confined': 'Parlours, sitting-rooms, halls, dining rooms, dens, all of them disappeared as such and were merged into one large living-space'.[7] Along with the disappearance of defined rooms we also witness the loss of secondary architectural elements: alcoves, closets, larders, hallways, fuel storage and built-in cupboards. Even the declining array of thresholds and subsequent diminishment of the door occurred without much resistance in the shift from the old world to the new world.

With these case study projects, we are seeing more than just a return of doors – each of the practices appears to be taking a leap beyond the notion of a door as an accidental feature of habitable space. The architects are treating the door as having an imminent logic of its own. The door is not simply a device at the service of architectural needs, but a frame for conceptualising how rooms relate to one another and how the interior relates to outdoor terraces or loggias. We could see this as a continuation of the position Robin Evans takes in his description of the Villa Madama's plan as a 'picture of social relations':

> First, the rooms have more than one door – some have two doors, many have three, others four – a feature which, since the early years

6 Robin Evans, 'Figures, Doors and Passages', in *Translations from Drawing to Building and Other Essays*, Architectural Association Publications, London, 2011 (1978), pp. 56–57.

7 Catherine Bauer, *Modern Housing*, The Riverside Press, Cambridge MA, 1934, p. 200.

> of the 19th century, has been regarded as a fault in domestic buildings of whatever kind or size. Why?[8]

Evans goes on to suggest that 'in 16th-century Italy a convenient room had many doors; in 19th-century England a convenient room had but one'. What he describes as 'thoroughfare rooms' suggest that 'there is no qualitative distinction between the way through the house and the inhabited spaces within it'.[9] These multiple routes do not favour any particular space, unlike corridors (passages) and their accompanying 'terminal rooms'. Similar approaches were favoured among the group of architects in the online discussion – the breaking down of hierarchies, the creation of shortcuts and enfilades, resulting in interesting spaces that are not so much determined by function but open to different interpretations.

Jeannette Kuo expands on this idea when discussing the organisational logic of the Cham Apartments, citing Robin Evans when describing the practice's approach. Kuo refers to 'two spatial anchors' that define two radically different ways of living. Kuo also refers to Berlin architect and planner Alexander Klein who was featured in the writings of both Evans and Bauer. Evans is very much a critic of Klein's work – in the words of Kuo, Evans was 'lamenting the overly determined plan'.

> In the 19th-century example, the 'necessary movements' of persons from room to room cross and intersect like rails in a shunting yard, but in the House for Frictionless Living they remain entirely distinct and do not touch at all; paths literally never cross. [...] The justification for Klein's plan was the metaphor hidden in its title, which implied that all accidental encounters caused friction and therefore threatened the smooth running of the domestic machine: a delicately balanced and sensitive device it was too, always on the edge of malfunction.[10]

Klein proposed in 1928 that the home should be designed to prevent the flow of inhabitants from crossing each other. 'The Functional House for Frictionless Living' was a series of pathway diagrams mapping the trajectories of daily life. The diagrams depicted a 'bad example' (J. J. P. Oud's apartment plan for his Weißenhofsiedlung on the left) and a 'good example' (Klein's plan for Berlin-Dahlem on the right), which were intended to avoid family conflicts by reducing the everyday confrontation with the other. Christoph Lueder, in his paper 'Evaluator, Choreographer, Ideologue,

8 Evans, 'Figures, Doors and Passages', p. 63.

9 Ibid, pp. 63–64.

10 Ibid, p. 85.

Catalyst' argues that the refinement of these diagrams was about separating out activities and not people, as many critics like Evans have proposed.[11] Lueder is suggesting that Klein's intent has been tangled up at 'the intersection of diverging functionalist strategies, critiques of functionalism, and reinterpretations of functionalism'.[12] However, he does acknowledge the significant impact these diagrams had on a generation of architects who declared that 'we can't make plans any better'.[13]

What Klein had in effect achieved was a pattern book. 'Various Solutions for a Floor Plan Drawn to the Same Scale for Exact Comparison and Evaluation' is a set of instructions and what we might now interpret as akin to a set of minimum standards for the profession and a guide to spatial decluttering. With the endorsement of influential housing scholars like Catherine Bauer, variations of Klein's apartment plans would go on to reshape mass housing across Europe and America.

Lueder notes in the same paper that 'Van Doesburg (1926) in his criticism of functionalism put forward a rejoinder against minimisation, advocating for what he called, redundant space, which he suggests, "we might not experience physically, but instead psychically and perhaps even more spiritually"'.[14] The idea of the frictionless house emerges again in Bachelard's *The Poetics of Space* and what he refers to as an 'oneiric house'. A house stripped of its attic and basement lacks 'intimacy'. In describing urban dwellings, Bachelard suggests that 'the inhabitants of the big city live in superimposed boxes', and have 'no roots' – their relation to space has become artificial.[15] The attic filled the pages of children's books as a space for the imagination, escape and adventure while supplying an answer to the practical need for storage.

My own experience – having been born and raised in a tenement flat – was that tenement alcoves (historically bed recesses), some with curtains, folding doors or screens, became the surrogate attic or cellar space – what Jeremy Till has referred to as slack space, 'allowing for difference and ambiguity to flourish'.[16] The alcove provided a space that wasn't fully determined – it was in Kuo's words 'malleable space', like a 19th-century hallway. The alcove could be storage, the place for an awkward sideboard, a piano, a child's cot, bunk beds, dining space or study. With the removal of an internal wall, the back-to-back alcoves became a primary element (a room), transforming from a slack space to what Till suggests is the 'hard space'. Modest in plan,

11 Christoph Lueder, 'Evaluator, Choreographer, Ideologue, Catalyst', *Journal of the Society of Architectural Historians*, 2017, 76, (1): pp. 82–106.

12 Ibid, p. 93.

13 Ibid, p. 94.

14 Ibid, p. 94. Lueder is quoting Van Doesburg from 'Defending the Spirit of Space: Against a Dogmatic Functionalism' (1926), in *On European Architecture: Complete Essays from Het Bouwbedriff 1924–1931*, Birkhäuser Verlag, Basel (Headquarters), 1990, p. 91.

15 Gaston Bachelard, *The Poetics of Space* (M. Jolas trans.), Beacon Press, Boston, 1994, pp. 26–27.

16 Adam Wood, 'Interview with Jeremy Till on Schools, Contingency, Flexibility and Competitions', *Architecture and Education*, 18 January 2018, accessed 18 January 2024. https://architectureandeducation.org/2018/01/18/interview-with-jeremy-till-on-schools-contingency-flexibility-and-competitions/

the alcove allowed for a certain spatial ambiguity and responsiveness to the activities of the occupants. Akin to Kiyonori Kikutake's Sky House with its kids' rooms, or 'move-nets' suspended under the floor, the tenement alcove addressed the changeability inherent in a single family.

What each of the case study plans demonstrates is several oscillating and sometimes contradictory readings of the same plan: as groups of spaces segregated from each other or as a matrix or grid of interconnected spaces. Like Klein's plans they invite competing diagrammatic annotation: explicit, deterministic pathways are set against an implicit matrix of possibilities – we can imagine ourselves as children exploiting all the possibilities of open-endedness, as adults rearranging the furniture in multiple configurations and as elderly ageing in the comfort of carefully choreographed spaces with views to a larger context.

Klein's notion that architecture might malfunction through improper use or arrangement of rooms suggests the plan is fixed and nothing is left to chance. In contrast, the unpredictable behaviour of people is the starting point for someone like Hermann Czech or Josef Frank. People and their behaviours are in fact the very artistic material of Czech's and Frank's architecture. We see parallels in approach with the case study plans presented in the symposium. The notion that architecture could be contaminated through use is far removed from the motivations of each of the architects featured in this publication.

Henri Lefebvre viewed the homogenising rationality of capitalism as a force that strips the 'living substance' from human interactions and thus 'leads to the impoverishment [...] of everyday life'.[17] Lefebvre would have rallied against Klein's sterilised plans and functionalist theories that found their way out into the planning of the 20th-century city. In contrast, these new plans acknowledge the role of social dynamics in the production of space and, consequently, facilitate a more meaningful spatial experience. Philipp Esch suggests that floor plans are a kind of connective tissue in the wider city: 'floor plans must have this tolerance to adapt to very different ways of life. [...] they have to be more open and less determined. Perhaps spatially quite determined, but functionally rather undetermined.' – open yet defined.[18]

In a way, the conceptual context for the plan is not finished with the completion of the built project. As Czech suggests, 'it can be spun on through the experiences that the inhabitants have with the building'.[19] The plan

17 Michel Trebitsch, preface to *Critique of Everyday Life: Volume 1*, Verso, London, 1991, p. xxiii.

18 Ana Catarina Silva, 'Housing. Not Flats. A Conversation with Philipp Esch', *Daidalos*, 18 January 2024, accessed 18 January 2024. https://www.daidalos.org/de/artikel/esch

19 Kuss, *Hermann Czech*, p. 150.

is only there at the end of a process, at the end of a series of decisions. The addition of furniture will then generate another spatial layer and atmosphere, again reinforcing the idea of architecture as background. ‘Five Good Swiss Plans’ speaks explicitly to the freedom of the user and their active engagement with the architecture. Each plan has an ambiguity that will be appropriated over time. The undetermined space is not left void but carefully designed and prepared for residents to assert control. As Czech declared, ‘architectural intervention is only strong when it is binding; arbitrariness ends in redundancy and boredom’.[20]

20 Ibid, p. 384.

Towards the end of the 19th century, Swiss cities grew very quickly. The entrepreneurs who developed housing at this time were also involved in their construction. The housing they built, called *Baumeisterhäuser*, followed catalogue-like templates, with robust floor plans that functioned regardless of location or orientation. Their façades were unadorned but well proportioned, while their simple structures could be erected without special instruction. The *Baumeisterhäuser* formed larger neighbourhoods and are still popular today because their neutrality allows for a wide variety of uses and living constellations. Despite their generic character, such type-houses achieve a lot: multiple houses can create attractive places with a surprisingly high density.[1] However, the *Baumeisterhaus* type is a passive participant in the urban scene, as it displaces space instead of framing it.

In our own practice, the planning of such type-houses is the exception. We prefer to plan buildings that interact with the site. We want to bring order and structure into the field of tension between the different forces of the city. We use the construction of housing as a pretext for conceiving urban spaces where people choose to meet and spend time. Housing is a volume with which we can create a setting, a frame.

But dwellings are not simply benign structures made up of rooms. Just as the plan of the city is a mapping of social events, so too the floor plans of dwellings are mappings of life, of everyday, bodily and concrete activities. Within dwellings, social and cultural habits, desires for sentimentality and security, but also mundane ergonomics, hygiene and technical efficiency come together. When individual dwellings are combined, the result is an abstract texture, a crystalline-like structure. This dichotomy of concreteness on a micro level and abstraction on a macro level is fascinating. It keeps us interested in the design of housing.

All the apartments we design are for rent. We do not design apartments to buy. As a result, no one owns the walls they live in. Rental dwellings are more generic as they are not tailored to the whims and tastes of their owners. This is a privilege for the architect, but it also comes with the challenge of creating spaces that are non-specific and suitable to many people. In this sense, the task of housing is to balance a strong spatial determinacy with an indeterminacy of use.

We were invited to plan two houses for a site on the edge of Bern.[2] The development is in the new Schönberg-Ost district and is based on a master plan by Hans Kollhoff. The basic

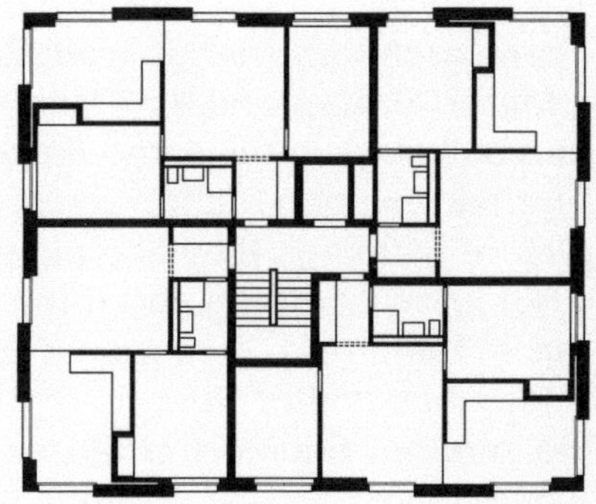

Apartment Building with Seasons Room, Typical plan, 1:400

1 [EDITOR'S NOTE] The *Baumeisterhaus* (master builder's house) is a detached suburban housing typology from the 1830-1890s that coincided with an immigration and construction boom in Zurich. The term *Baumeisterhäuser* characterises their authors, being master builders with craftsmen roots. It is not a housing for a bourgeois client and is therefore more modest, containing both apartments and workshops. In his presentation, Esch noted a fascination with the robustness and clarity of these plans which explains the pursuit of a strong spatial determinacy in his own work. See *Zürcher Baumeisterhäuser: Zeugen einer wachsenden Stadt. Verkannte Architektur aus dem 19. Jahrhundert,* Stadt, Zurich, 2011.

urban design is an arrangement of urban villas, a typology from the 1980s, with two dwellings per floor. Three architect friends from Bern, Thomas Pulver, Marco Graber and Rolf Mühlethaler, had designed buildings in the same development. Being in their company flattered us. We knew what kind of buildings they had planned, but we did not know anything about the other buildings in the street. In response, we decided to develop houses that were as regular as possible, modern *Baumeisterhäuser* so to speak. They would have to resist potentially unfriendly neighbouring houses across the street and be able to withstand the predetermined narrow spacing between houses. One house was to be tailored to a wealthy tenant segment with larger space requirements, the other was to become a prototype for a newly founded real estate fund dedicated to affordable housing.

This economic difference became the catalyst for the development of the two houses. In the cheap house we accommodated four flats per floor; in the expensive house only two. In the expensive house, each flat has three balconies; in the cheap house there are none. The flats in the expensive house culminate in their centre, a living hall, while those in the cheap house do so at their edge, in a kitchen on the corners of each floor. The expensive flats have a centripetal and introverted plan, the cheap ones are centrifugal and extroverted.[3]

The affordable housing had a limited budget, but thriftiness can only be tolerated if it is contrasted with lavishness. The costs saved by omitting balconies were allocated to very large sliding windows, which turned the kitchen into a seasonal room.[4] The tiles on the floor and the trellis on the façade (which we hope will eventually be planted) contribute to the room's character as an outdoor space.

The real protagonists of the building are the generous sliding windows, which add a theatrical and sumptuous moment to a low-cost house. When open, the windows slide into a wall cavity, leaving the interior undisturbed. The result is a thickened wall that is read in the façade as a sculptural vertical division. In this way, the sliding windows also become key elements in the building's external expression.

Philipp Esch

2 [EDITOR'S NOTE] Swiss architects refer to multi-residential housing as a house, singular. This could be attributed to the influence of Diener & Diener (The House and the City), but such an idea is also reflected in typologies such as: the *Baumeisterhaus* (master builder's house), *Mehrfamilienhaus* (multi-family house) and *Stadtvilla* (urban villa). We think this gives housing a unified quality, emphasising the building as a singular and cohesive figure rather than emphasising individual units which became the norm in Australian residential development following the introduction of the *Strata Titles Act 1961* (NSW).

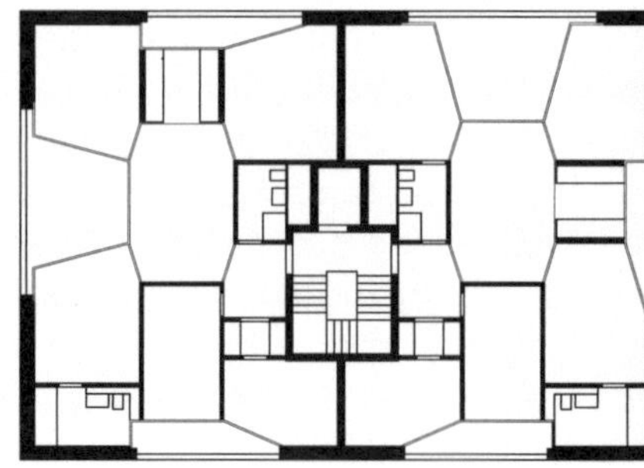

Apartment Building with Central Hall, Typical plan, 1:400

'Room with no name'. Wurster, Bernardi and Emmons, Wurster House, Stinson Beach, California, 1962. Photograph by Morley Baer. Source: Marc Treib, *An Everyday Modernism: The Houses of William Wurster*, University of California Press, Berkeley, 1995, p. 69

3 [EDITOR'S NOTE] The apartment plans of Esch Sintzel and Conen Sigl originally included a secondary route around the periphery of the apartment that was not built. In his presentation, Esch mentioned that this secondary path allowed for less hierarchy in circulation, and that its removal had the effect of making the living room more central, with all access set in relation to it. Padmanabhan and Kuo also spoke of an enjoyment for this secondary route in the pursuit of a less hierarchical inhabitation of their plans.

4 [EDITOR'S NOTE] The 'seasonal room' is also referred to by Esch as an 'all seasons room' or *Küchenloggia* (balcony kitchen).

[00:20:02] We wanted to do without balconies because they are the most expensive area to construct and they lead to a reduction in rentable floor area. Instead, we looked to superimpose functions like the bathroom, which serves as a corridor, and the balcony, which doubles as a kitchen.

The seasons room reminded me of a wonderful anecdote by Grete Tugendhat describing how it felt in deep winter when they would lower the window panes in the Villa Tugendhat and sit in a wonderful Mies Van der Rohe living room but would be sitting outside in the snow at the same time.* We wanted to make everything in this room feel as outside as possible. We also had in mind the 'room with no name', a term coined by the Californian architect William Wurster.

* '...that on sunny winter days, even at very low temperatures, we never had to heat the downstairs room and could even lower the large window panes electrically and then sit as if outdoors.' Grete Tugendhat, 'Zum Bau des Hauses Tugendhat' in *Bauwelt*, 1969, 36: p.1246.

[00:21:25] The plan was very simple. Within each apartment, the structure of the rooms is set by the volume of the kitchen and the bathroom. We particularly liked that you would be able to circulate freely around this fixed core, but that you had two very different ways of circulating: one, a very long way along the façade and the other, a shortcut through the bathroom. It reminds me of the Milanese architect Luigi Caccia Dominioni who argued for the informal, purely functional connections to be as short as possible and the long formal, representative connections as long as possible.†

One thing that is very dear to us is to have an articulated threshold between the collective and the private world. As a result, you do not enter the apartment directly, but instead there is a small room between the shared staircase and your living room.

† 'Caccia always endeavoured to work out 'minimal distances for strictly functional connections (for example from the kitchen to the dining room)' in order to give the 'so-called representative sections maximum development'. See Luigi Caccia Dominioni in conversation with Eugenio Gentili in *Arbitare*, 1963, 13, quoted in: Astrid Staufer, 'Hierarchische Konkurrenz', in *Werk, Bauen + Wohnen*, 1996, 5: pp.26-35, here p.32.

For the past decade in Swiss housing, there has been a focus on rethinking the apartment plan. The question of how an apartment can be organised internally has been the focus of many projects. As a result, apartments have often been developed following the structural logic of modernist estates, with ideal apartment plans grouped into buildings, and buildings arranged into *Siedlungen* (estates).

In our Herdernstrasse apartment building we tried to invert the structural logic of modernist housing by looking at the apartment as a quintessentially urban plan.

The building forms a bookend to an incomplete urban block, the last on Zurich's western edge. Positioned at the end of a dense 19th-century working-class area, the site gives way to urban sprawl, which stretches into the depths of the Limmat Valley. The tough character of the context is reinforced by the presence of a slaughterhouse and a soccer stadium nearby, two heroic elements of the industrial city. The centre of the block contains a large field of allotment gardens.

We conceived of the building as having two distinct façades. The street façade is rusticated with a sturdy relief made of fibre cement panels, while the façade facing the allotment gardens is a rendered lightweight skin, as thin as an eggshell.

On the inside, the apartment plans have an ambiguous character that oscillates between a Loosian *Raumplan* and an open plan, reminiscent of Le Corbusier. When the internal doors remain open during the day, the space feels fluid. At night, when the doors are closed, the spatial order transforms into something more composite and cellular.

The apartment's internal structure is defined by precast concrete pillars with thin walls and full-height doors that appear as membranes, connecting the dots of the pillars in plan. These rectangular columns define the orientation of the apartment and its relationship to the exterior. Towards the street, their alignment is parallel to the façade, protecting the interior from the immense space of the sprawling Limmat Valley. Towards the courtyard, the pillars are rotated 90 degrees, thus drawing the green space of the allotment gardens into the interior.

The apartment works like the lungs of a human body. Inhaling, the urban space enters the dwelling. Exhaling, the view leads us outward, across the urban landscape.

Thomas Padmanabhan and Oliver Lütjens

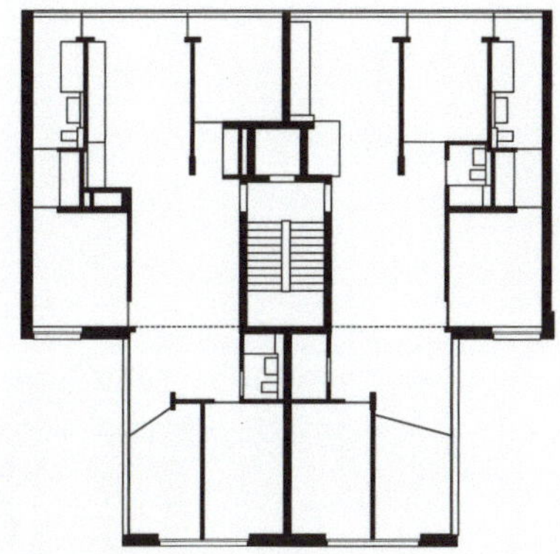

Herdernstrasse Apartments, Level 2-3 plan, 1:400

Herdernstrasse Apartments, Photograph by Walter Mair

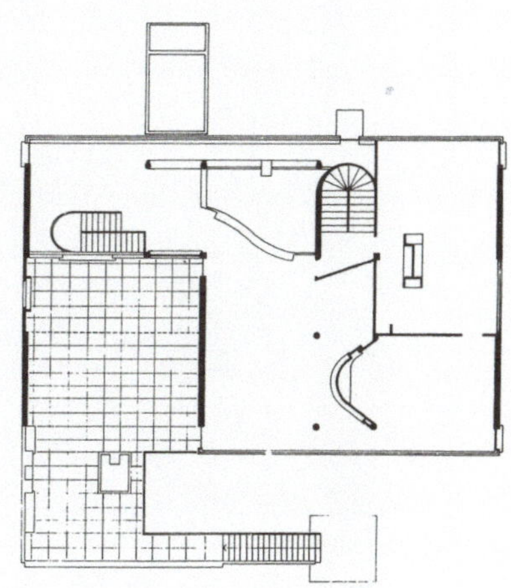

Le Corbusier, Villa Stein-de-Monzie, Garches, Level 1 plan, 1927. Source: Adapted from Colin Rowe, *The Mathematics of the Ideal Villa and Other Essays*, The MIT Press, Cambridge MA, 1976, p.21. © FLC. ADAGP/Copyright Agency, 2025

HORNBACH
650 x 350 x 370mm

[00:40:13] You can see a figure in the apartments that combines the main living room on the courtyard side with a bathroom on the street. One of the main reasons for doing this was that although we enjoy the circular path that you could take around these apartments at night or day, crossing the kitchen, going into the bathroom, entering through the wardrobe into the bedroom and so on, but at the same time, street noise laws for bedrooms were very strict, so we brought the bathroom to the street.

[00:43:31] We wanted the spatial structure to oscillate between a cellular plan, a Loosian idea of space and a free-flowing open plan like Le Corbusier. We thought to do this by emphasising the load-bearing quality of the columns and by weaving the walls and doors between them. During the day, the doors can be opened, leaving free-standing walls, with the space flowing around them (especially along the street façade). At night all of the doors can be closed, which would result in a series of private rooms. The inspiration for the dialogue between these elements can be seen in a plan of Villa Garches by Le Corbusier of 1927 where there is an ambiguous relationship between pillars and walls.

There are pillars that are free-standing and those that are connected to walls and they have a very complex relationship that was really inspiring for us. In reality the space is less structured and more free-flowing in three dimensions than is revealed in the plan.

[00:46:32] On either side of the pillars, you can see the continuity of space but you can also see the manipulation and limits of the views created by doors, which are sometimes closed. With doors you can regulate the openness of the spatial structure very precisely. There is an enfilade along the street façade that connects the living room, a bedroom and the bathroom.

To begin with, a short detour.

Architecture is about considering the world in spatial terms, from immense landscapes down to the smallest areas at the scale of furniture. Each provokes questions and has its own richness.

Architecture is about making rooms and habitats as diverse and multi-layered as possible. It is not only about the habitats of humans, but also that of plants, trees, insects, bees, birds and other living creatures.

Architecture is about creating ecological spaces. Due to intense urbanisation and the destruction of natural environments, we need to create refuges for living creatures. Our aim is to foster projects where natural and built space co-exist.

Architecture is also about creating less defined spaces, where use is unprescribed.

Finally, architecture brings cohesion to these spaces through a project and a plan.

One project that attempts to weave these elements together is located on the outskirts of Zurich in the Hochbord neighbourhood, which is currently undergoing profound changes. Significant land damage has occurred over time in this former industrial area, which has been rezoned as residential. In 2017, the landowner, together with a housing cooperative (WOGENO), organised an architecture competition for a housing project. The subsequent Hochbord Dübendorf is situated on land that was previously used as a plant nursery.

The project is divided into three parts. At the front is a community centre, a rotated volume, which faces a pedestrian street and opens the block to the neighbourhood. A low, narrow linear slab of studio units follows the trainline and shields the apartments (housed in the largest building) from the noise of the trainline. With its roof terrace and trellis, the studio building helps to give the project an identity that recalls the site's past as a nursery. The largest slab, along the east, contains the residential units and overlooks the studio building with views to the surrounding landscape. The three building volumes follow the perimeter of the site and create a quiet communal courtyard in the centre.

The building volumes form outdoor spaces of different qualities, from the very public to the very private. They include the square around the community centre, the large central courtyard between the two housing slabs, a roof terrace and private balconies. Between and within these spaces several bird houses are planned. Birds and people will live side by side.

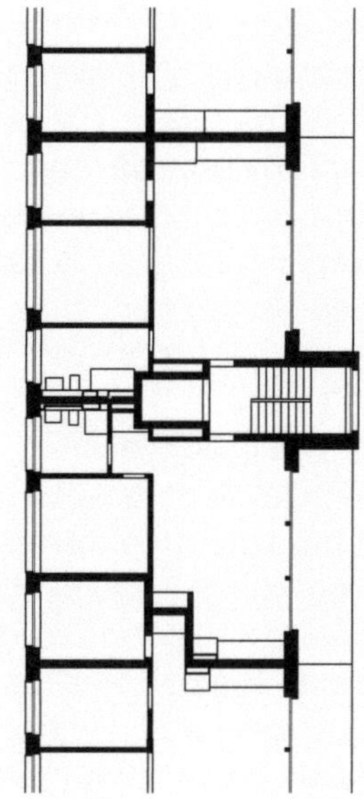

Westhof Dübendorf, Level 5–8 plan, 1:400

Westhof Dübendorf, Photograph by Philip Heckhausen

On the lower levels of the main residential slab, the floor plan is deeper. At the centre of each apartment is a large hall, around which all the functions are organised. The private rooms are along the eastern façade, and different door openings connect these rooms to the hall. A middle room, which is an extension of the hall, is directly connected to it via a large, hinged double door.[1] The kitchen and the living room are oriented towards the balcony that faces the main central courtyard.

The fifth level connects the roof terraces across buildings via an external stair. This level includes rooms that are available for inhabitants and complements the rooms of their apartment. These so-called 'flex rooms' can be rented for a short time, even for a few hours, to be used as music rooms or coworking spaces.

On the uppermost levels, the slab gets thinner. Here the units are defined by the character of living between two façades. The private rooms are repeated along the east façade and the living areas are along the west. Within the apartment you always have a direct connection to both façades of the building.[2]

Maria Conen

Westhof Dübendorf, Axonometric sketch

1 [EDITOR'S NOTE] The study of door sizes, position and their expression is a commonality between three of the five Swiss plans included in this publication. As these examples show, doors define how we move from one room to the next, and this is fundamental in determining a room's hierarchy and use.

2 [EDITOR'S NOTE] We have included the dwelling plan from the project's winning competition entry. We prefer this plan to what was built for its enfilade through rooms along the east façade.

[01:12:11] The double doors are a way of opening the middle room onto the living room. This room can be a bedroom, but you could also open the doors and use it as a study that becomes part of the main living space. Depending on the size of the doors, the rooms belong more or less together. The middle room might also be a children's room, from which toys could come in and out. Maybe it is to be thought of like the doors of a cupboard that can be opened or closed. When planning this project we wanted rooms of good proportions that could be regulated through different door openings: smaller doors offer more privacy and even if the door is left open, what is beyond is less visible.

There is also the question of how you furnish a plan and how many possibilities are available. An argument against multiple doors is always the flexibility of furnishing the room. If there are more pathways through a room you could imagine someone might say 'I can't put furniture there', or if the door is closed I think people cannot envision putting furniture against it.

You could say that any floor plan is the negotiation between the external constraints of a site and the internal logic of inhabitation, but this is particularly true of the project in Cham. Given the tiny triangular site, it was important to be resourceful with every square metre. We were interested in understanding the possible organisational logics within this geometry even though it could only accommodate two average-sized apartments on each floor. We wanted to come up with living experiences that would capitalise on the triangular form rather than fight against it. This meant that we had to contend with two units atypical of market housing: a very narrow and pointed unit, and an exceptionally deep unit.

The biggest challenge for the deep unit was to find an organisational logic that would take advantage of its geometry. We sought a logic that would seem almost natural to the depth while maximising its spatial value. A non-hierarchical collection of rooms offered such a possibility. The cellular divisions allowed us to negotiate the idiosyncrasies of the site and code constraints while maintaining an overall integrity.

The deep unit is characterised by a central hall, a room that is more typical of 18th- and 19th-century aristocratic homes than it is of modern housing, but a space that we found fascinating in its potential.[1] The hall replaces the usual mono-functional corridor with a usable, multi-functional space. However, instead of the monumentality of its historical precedents, the central hall in Cham is non-hierarchical and democratic. This is the centre of life in the apartment, a space which is undetermined and open to interpretation. The central hall is a space where everyone meets or crosses paths, but it is also a space that retreats from the exterior, a space only for the inhabitants. Although caught within the centre of the plan, it is unexpectedly porous and dynamic with light and views in all directions. We liked the hall's ambiguity: it is simultaneously transitional and a point of stasis; both centrifugal and centripetal.

The loggia gives the central hall its sense of porosity and lightness, but also a calming sense of protection through the layering of space. Because of the building's proximity to the railroad, each room has indirect access to the exterior through a loggia, which also fulfils the requirements of acoustic comfort. It became an opportunity to rethink the relationship of inside and outside through a mid-space, an outdoor room that reinforces the logic of the plan, without which the deep centre could not be inhabited. For us the plan is a conceptual

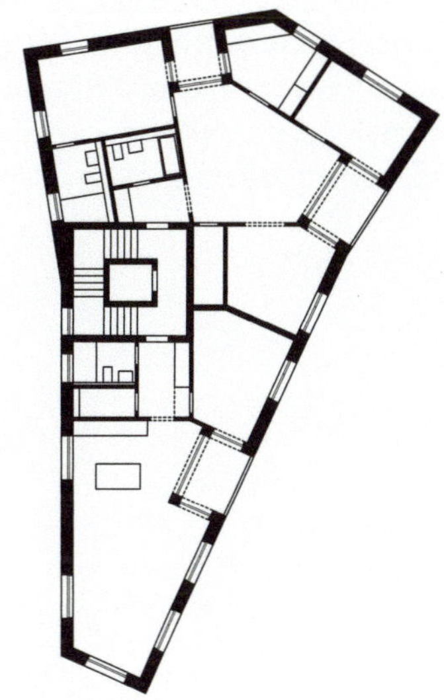

Cham Apartments, Level 2 plan, 1:400

1 [EDITOR'S NOTE] A central entry is also seen in the Herdernstrasse project by Lütjens Padmanabhan. Stephen Bates has detailed his interest in the central entry nicely in S. Bates, 'Living from the Centre', in *Papers 3: Sergison Bates Architects*, Quart Publishers, Lucerne, 2016, pp.108–121.

Cham Apartments, Photograph by Rory Gardiner

tool for thinking organisationally. It sets up spatial and programmatic relationships through a formal order. But in the end, it's an abstraction, something we never experience in totality – a logic perceived not in two dimensions but as a dynamic spatial sequence.

Jeannette Kuo

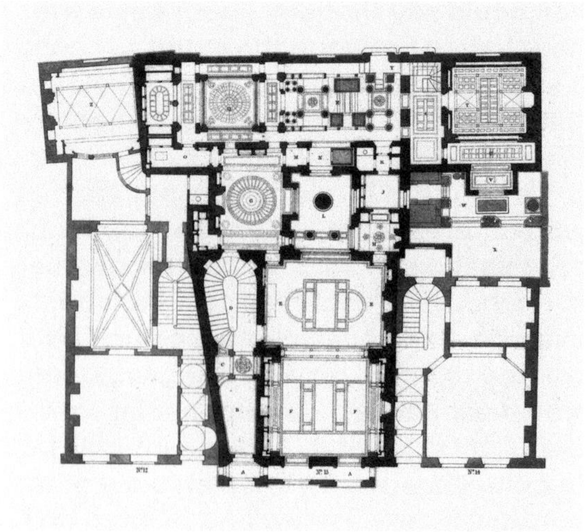

John Soane, Sir John Soane's Museum, Plan of the Ground or Hall Floor, 1833. Source: Adapted from Sir John Soane, *Description of the House and Museum on the North Side of Lincoln's Inn Fields*, London, 1835, p.3

FAIRY
FAIRY

[01:44:49] We were interested in the idea of a collection of spaces not so much determined by function but open to different interpretations, spaces that were connected in different ways and could have a softer hierarchy. If we think of a collection of spaces, there is no better example than Sir John Soane's house and his Bank of England scheme. Projects whose plans essentially negotiate the idiosyncrasies of the existing site but still preserve the distinct spatial characters of each space. In this case the hall and the stair become the kind of malleable spaces that allow the dining room and the library to remain platonic geometries.

In the Cham project, you can see that the rooms are in each case accessible not only from the central hall but also from the two rooms that flank it. This could become a shortcut from one room to another without ever having to cross the central hall.

[01:46:12] You enter the apartment through a vestibule into a hall in the middle of the plan where there is no prescribed directionality. You would feel protected, deep in the building but somehow still connected to the outside and in the centre of the action. This central hall is a room that is open for interpretation. We liked this ambiguity of it being simultaneously transitional as well as a point of stasis. Some people have used the hall as a dining room but it is large enough for kids to play in, to be a living space or even a combination of living and dining in order to gain an extra bedroom space.

Why the plan?
I would like to make some observations about thinking and designing in plan. For that which 'connects thinking to imagination, imagination to drawing, drawing to building, and buildings to our eyes' is already inherent in the technique and materiality of plan drawing.[1]

What is a plan? Descriptive geometry defines the plan as an orthogonal projection of a spatial object. In architecture, we define it as the projection of a horizontal section through a building at approximately eye level. As Robin Evans astutely states, the plan's connection to the ground is etymologically anchored in the words 'ground plan', *Grundriss, pianta*, and even 'platform'.[2] The plan reveals the interior of a building – it compels our gaze to consider the dissected body from above. It is fitting that this view has been compared to a divine insight, as the plan reveals a privileged view that would otherwise remain unseen. The plan is all-embracing because it includes not just the whole, but also the detail. There are no limits to the abundance of information presented in a plan. Yet the plan also suffices with limited graphic means, namely lines and surfaces.

Like a map, the plan is simultaneously abstract and representational. Abstract, because it depicts and formalises space geometrically – it is undistorted and true to scale. But it is also representational: it can convey a subjective spatial notion, even atmosphere, to the reader.

What arouses our interest when looking at, for example, a plan by Carlo Scarpa, is the beauty of the drawing, its colourfulness and material presence, the proportions, the geometric system and correlations that have led to its complexity, and last but not least, its legibility.

Floor Plan as Battle Plan (Le Corbusier)
In his 1923 text *Vers Une Architecture*, Le Corbusier wrote, 'But the plan is the generator, "the plan determines everything; it is an austere abstraction, an algebrization dry to the eye." It is a plan of battle. The battle ensues, and that is the great moment.'[3]

This outlines the primacy of the plan for Le Corbusier with regard to architectural drawings. This paradigm suggests a certain conception of space, that is, of a space that expands horizontally between horizontal planes. Vertical walls, which are an obstacle to this spatial expansion, may be avoided. The use of a steel skeleton structure not only optically enhances the impression of horizontal expansion but is also the structural prerequisite for this spatial notion. In such a horizontally conceived

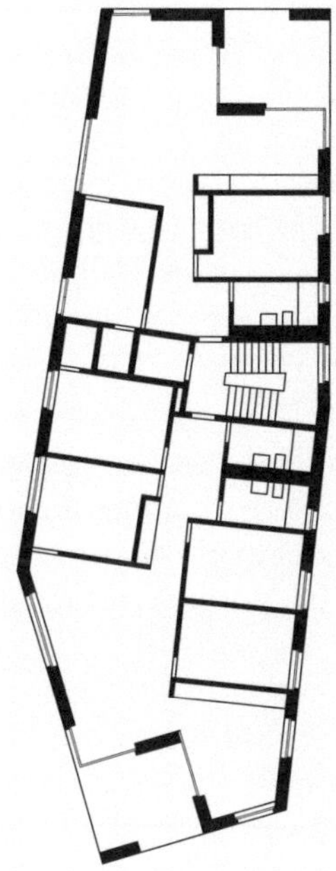

Katzenbach IV, Standard floor, Type I, 1:400

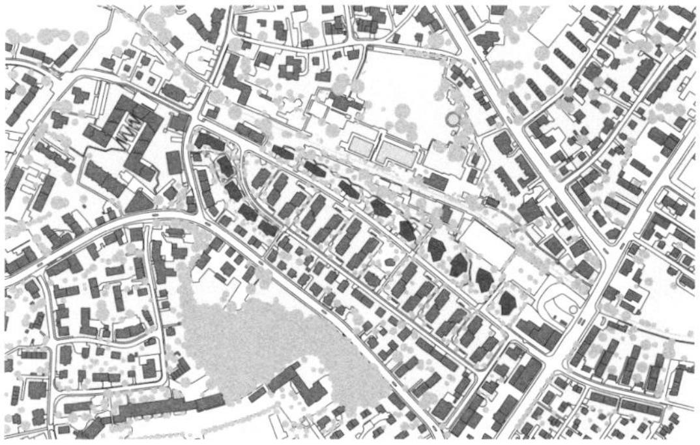

Katzenbach IV, Context plan

1 Robin Evans, 'Introduction: Composition and Projection', in *The Projective Cast: Architecture and Its Three Geometries*, The MIT Press, Cambridge, MA, 1995, p. xxxi.
2 Ibid, p. 113.

3 Le Corbusier, *Toward an Architecture*, trans. John Goodman, Getty Research Institute, Los Angeles, 2007, p. 215.

spatial arrangement, the plan drawing reveals everything. The horizontal section at eye level reveals the intrinsic organisational structure of the whole, its logic, its programmatic and spatial relationships.

Another consequence of the primacy of the plan is the fact that buildings are designed from the inside out. Le Corbusier underscores this aspect when he polemically states, 'A building is like a soap bubble. [...] The exterior is the result of an interior.'[4]

The shift from the façade to the plan marks a decisive change in direction that modern architecture took at the end of the 19th and the beginning of the 20th century. Prior to this, as with 18th-century classicism for example, the battlefield was not the floor plan, but the front elevation. Thus, the internal spatial disposition was subordinated to the symmetrical arrangement of the façade. The building was designed from the outside in. To take this approach to its logical conclusion, one could say that interior spaces were the structural framework that supported the façade. The modernist shift, on the other hand, is encapsulated by the terms 'composing' and 'projecting'.[5] Whereas composition assembles existing elements into a new whole, the projection has an open outcome.

Plan as Notation and Narration of a Way of Life

The supremacy of the plan led to its formal liberation. Walls no longer had to conform to the order of an obligatory principle of structure and construction in order to create a certain expression on the façade. Thus, the plan – liberated, individual and expressive – became a notation and projection of a possible way of life. The plan could be developed situationally, reflecting the needs of its occupants and the ideals of the architect. With the arrival of this moment, the 'narrative' entered the plan. The floor plan became 'readable', a text about what could be experienced. The plan was subsequently overlaid with a composed dramaturgy about the paths, sequences, experiences and events possible within the space.[6]

In our architectural practice, the plan assumes the most important role among the three types of projections. From the initial idea and the first hand-drawn sketch to design development and construction drawings with CAD software, we use the plan to indicate preliminary spatial configurations and concepts, or to grasp programmatic complexity to document for

4 Ibid, p. 216.

5 Ákos Moravánsky, 'Die Geste des Komponierens' (The Gesture of Composing), *trans*, 2011, 19: pp. 36–47.

6 [EDITOR'S NOTE] Unsurprisingly the work of Luigi Caccia Dominioni is cited as an influence by a number of the architects included in this publication. Dominioni saw the architect's primary interest in the development of the floor plan to be the 'telling of a story' ('*raccontare una storia*'). Astrid Staufer, 'Hierarchische Konkurrenz', in *Werk, Bauen + Wohnen*, 1996, 5: pp. 26–35, here p. 31. See also Elli Mosayebi, 'Konstruktionen von Ambiente: Wohnungsbau von Luigi Caccia Dominioni in Mailand, 1945-1970,' PhD diss., ETH Zurich, 2014.

construction. The plan is exceedingly important, whether as a working tool in the design process or as a medium for representing the project.

The plan's importance in architecture is constantly being undermined. Architecture is increasingly seen as an object of consumption. The separation into core and shell has become a practice in which the exterior is subordinate to the conditions of the market and the interior is relinquished to maximum arbitrariness.

We understand the architect's work on plans as an opportunity to exercise resistance against these homogenising economic forces and consequently, against trivial and iconic architecture. In the plan, as a conveyor of structural and functional relationships, the architectural object becomes comprehensible as a coherent whole.

Elli Mosayebi

Katzenbach IV, Photograph by Roland Bernath

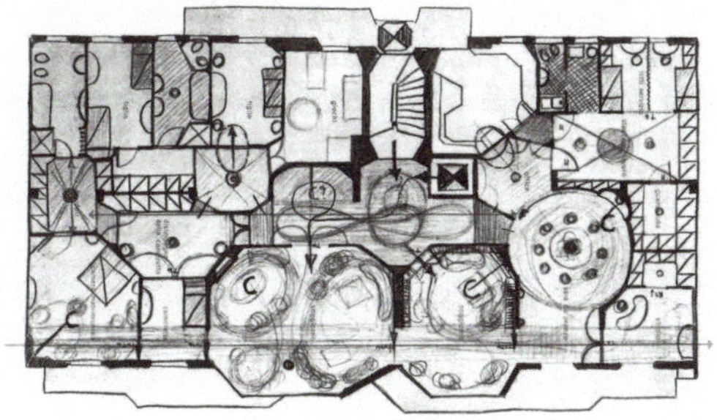

Luigi Caccia Dominioni, Via Vigoni 13, Milan, Level 4 plan sketch, 1959. Source: Adapted from Luigi Caccia Dominioni, arch., 'A Milano, una casa ad appartamenti', *Domus*, 1961, 380: p. 38

[02:04:51] Caccia Dominioni's work on the floor plan has been extremely important for his oeuvre but also for us as architects. In the beautiful sketch of Via Vigoni you can see the primacy of the floor plan is outlined, where he seeks with lines to anticipate the movement of the future dweller so you see the crossing lines in the floor plan that somehow also create space, and he designs the spaces to reflect this anticipation.

[02:17:48] From the entrance hall, the space is squeezed, and then it opens again into a kitchen niche where there is a corner window with a view towards the outside. Then you have the living room and a small door that leads to an extra room, which can be a library or a third room. The loggia is extremely important as it is the end point of the passage through the apartment.

We also wanted to emphasise the different perspectives that you would enjoy as you passed through the apartment, almost as though you are a flâneur walking through your own dwelling enjoying different views.